500

OF THE GREATEST
GOLF FACTS

First Published in 2023

History of Golf

Golf's origins trace back to Scotland in the 15th century, though similar games were played in the Netherlands earlier.

The game was initially banned by the Scottish Parliament in 1457 because it distracted from military training.

The first documented evidence of golf is King James II's prohibition of the game in 1457.

St Andrews, established in 1552, is known as the "Home of Golf."

The Old Course at St Andrews is considered the oldest golf course in the world.

The standard 18-hole course was established at St Andrews in 1764.

The first known rules of golf were written in 1744 for the Company of Gentlemen Golfers, now the Honourable Company of Edinburgh Golfers.

The gutta-percha ball, or "guttie," introduced in 1848, replaced the feather-filled leather ball, significantly changing the game.

The first official golf tournament, The Open Championship, was played on October 17, 1860, at Prestwick Golf Club in Scotland.

The Amateur Championship, the oldest amateur golf tournament, began in 1885.

The United States Golf Association (USGA) was founded in 1894 to govern the game in the U.S. and Mexico.

The Professional Golfers' Association of America (PGA of America) was established in 1916.

The Masters Tournament, one of the four major championships in professional golf, was first played in 1934.

The Ryder Cup, a biennial match between teams from Europe and the United States, started in 1927.

Golf was removed from the Olympic Games after 1904 and did not return until 2016.

The first golf tee was patented in 1899 by George F. Grant, an African American dentist.

Steel-shafted clubs were legalized by the USGA in 1924, replacing hickory shafts and transforming the game.

The first televised golf tournament was the 1954 U.S. Open.

The Royal and Ancient Golf Club of St Andrews (R&A) was formed in 1754 and is one of the oldest golf societies.

The term "birdie" comes from an American slang term from the late 19th century, meaning "something good."

The first 18-hole course in the United States was the Chicago Golf Club, founded in 1893.

The golf ball has undergone significant transformations, from wooden balls to featheries, gutties, and finally to the modern dimpled design.

The dimpled design of golf balls was patented in 1905, improving aerodynamics.

The modern golf bag with a stand was invented by Bruce Williamson in 1986.

Golf carts were introduced in the 1930s, initially powered by electricity.

The term "caddie" derives from the French word "cadet," meaning a younger child or a student military officer.

Golf gloves became popular in the 1890s to provide a better grip.

The first women's golf tournament was held in 1811 at Musselburgh, Scotland.

The LPGA (Ladies Professional Golf Association) was founded in 1950.

Golf entered Asia in the early 20th century, with the Royal Calcutta Golf Club (founded in 1829) being the oldest golf club outside the British Isles.

Ping introduced perimeter-weighted clubs in the 1960s, revolutionizing club design.

The first golf instruction book, "The Goff," was written by Thomas Kincaid in 1687.

Titanium drivers were introduced in the 1990s, allowing for larger clubheads and greater distances.

The Rules of Golf have been jointly governed by the R&A and the USGA since 1952.

The first recorded hole-in-one was made by Tom Morris at the Open Championship in Prestwick, Scotland, in 1868.

The concept of the handicap was introduced in 1911 to level the playing field among golfers of varying abilities.

Golf was first played in the United States in 1888, with the establishment of the St. Andrew's Golf Club in Yonkers, New York.

Arnold Palmer is credited with popularizing and commercializing golf in the 20th century, though we're focusing not on players.

The Solheim Cup, the women's equivalent of the Ryder Cup, was established in 1990.

Golf's inclusion in the 2016 Olympics marked the sport's return after a 112-year absence.

The longest golf course in the world is the International Golf Club in Massachusetts, stretching over 8,300 yards.

The concept of the "mulligan," or do-over, is believed to have originated in the 1920s but is not recognized in official rules.

The 1930s saw the rise of metal club heads, though wooden heads remained popular until the late 20th century.

The Haskell ball, invented in 1898, was the first rubber-cored ball, significantly affecting distance and flight.

In 2004, the USGA limited the maximum velocity and distance a golf ball can achieve.

The PGA TOUR was established as a separate entity from the PGA of America in 1968, focusing on organizing professional tournament golf.

The "Stimpmeter," a device to measure the speed of golf greens, was introduced in 1935.

The Green Jacket of the Masters Tournament, awarded to the winner since 1949, is one of golf's most iconic symbols.

The "19th hole" is slang for the clubhouse or bar where golfers go to relax after a round.

The creation of golf simulators in the late 20th century allowed for the game to be played virtually, promoting its growth.

Golf's first known match was between James IV of Scotland and the Earl of Bothwell in 1503.

The featherie ball, used before the gutta-percha, was so expensive because it was handcrafted with goose feathers tightly packed into a leather pouch.

In 1860, Prestwick Golf Club's Open Championship had only 8 competitors.

The term "bogey" originally referred to the ideal score for a skilled golfer, before "par" became the standard term.

Par was established as a term in golf scoring by the USGA in 1911, standardizing the number of strokes a skilled golfer should take to complete a hole.

The first recorded instance of golf in America was in 1657 in Charleston, South Carolina, when the city passed a law against playing golf in the streets.

The oldest golf tournament in North America is the Canadian Open, first played in 1904.

In 1922, Walter Hagen became the first native-born American to win the British Open.

The Royal Liverpool Golf Club, founded in 1869, was the first club in England to host The Open Championship.

The Saint Andrew's Golf Club in New York, established in 1888, is considered the oldest continuously operating golf club in the United States.

The first golf balls were made of wood, likely in the 14th century, and were used in the game's earliest forms.

Golf's first Olympic appearance was at the 1900 Paris Games.

The first hole-in-one on a par-4 in PGA TOUR history was achieved by Andrew Magee in 2001.

The youngest golfer to shoot a hole-in-one was reportedly 5 years old.

The largest golfing green is over 28,000 square feet, found at the 695-yard, 5th hole, a par 6 at the International Golf Club in Massachusetts.

The concept of the golf tee dates back to the late 19th century, but players initially just used mounds of sand.

The first driving range is thought to have been in Pinehurst, North Carolina, in the early 20th century.

Ben Hogan is famous for revolutionizing golf swing theory and practice.

The "Dimples" on golf balls vary in number, but a common configuration is 336 dimples.

The term "eagle" originated in the early 20th century as a continuation of the bird theme, representing a score one better than a "birdie."

Golf was initially played on public land where livestock often roamed, leading to the term "links," derived from the Old English word "hlinc," meaning rising ground or ridge.

The first 600 years of golf saw no standardized equipment, leading to significant variations in balls and clubs.

Aluminium putters introduced in the early 20th century marked the beginning of modern putter design.

Gene Sarazen invented the modern sand wedge in 1932, which greatly improved players' ability to escape sand traps.

The first recorded women's golf tournament took place in Musselburgh on January 9, 1811.

The Solheim Cup was named after Karsten Solheim, a key figure in the development of modern golf clubs.

The first comprehensive set of golf rules was established in 1744 by the Company of Gentlemen Golfers, now known as The Honourable Company of Edinburgh Golfers.

The Prince of Wales (later King Edward VII) was the first royal to be officially involved in golf, becoming the patron of The Golf Club at Tenby in 1888.

The first African American golfer to play in the Masters was Lee Elder, in 1975.

The system of creating golf holes with a uniform par to represent the standard score was formalized in the early 20th century.

The first official golf instructor was Allan Robertson, considered by many as the world's first professional golfer.

In 1938, the USGA began testing golf balls and in 1942 standardized their size and weight.

Golf course architects began to emerge as a profession in the early 20th century, with figures like Donald Ross and Alistair Mackenzie.

The first nine-hole golf course in America was laid out on a sheep farm in Downers Grove, Illinois, in 1892.

The golf term "fore" is believed to have come from the military "beware before," used to warn fellow golfers of an incoming shot.

In 1951, the first golf carts were introduced for people with disabilities, but they quickly became popular with all golfers.

The longest putt ever recorded in a tournament was 375 feet by Fergus Muir in 2001.

The first mention of golf in literature appears in a 1457 Scottish statute banning the game; the next was in a 1470 poem attributed to King James II.

The oldest "new" golf course is the Musselburgh Links, established in 1672, but golf was played on the site as early as 1567.

The US Open was established in 1895, one day after the first US Amateur Championship.

Tom Morris Jr., son of Old Tom Morris, won The Open Championship four times before his death at age 24.

In 1962, Jack Nicklaus won the U.S. Open, his first professional tournament win, marking the start of one of golf's greatest careers.

The first golf instruction book, "The Goff," written by Thomas Kincaid, was rediscovered in the 20th century, providing insights into early golf techniques.

Augusta National Golf Club, home of the Masters Tournament, was founded by Bobby Jones and Clifford Roberts and opened in 1933.

The Ryder Cup was originally a competition between the United States and Great Britain. It expanded to include Europe in 1979, dramatically increasing its competitiveness.

In the 1980s, metal woods began to replace traditional wooden woods, leading to significant changes in how the game was played.

The PGA European Tour was established in 1972, formalizing professional golf tours in Europe.

The Walker Cup, established in 1922, is a competition between amateur golfers from the U.S. and Great Britain & Ireland.

In 2014, the R&A voted to allow women members for the first time in its 260-year history.

The original 13 rules of golf included stipulations for how to deal with playing balls from watery ditches, stakes, and rabbit holes, reflecting the rudimentary and challenging conditions of early .

Famous Golfers

Tiger Woods made a televised appearance putting against comedian Bob Hope on "The Mike Douglas Show" at just 2 years old.

Bobby Jones is the only golfer ever to win the Grand Slam, capturing all four major championships in a single calendar year (1930).

Arnold Palmer was a pilot and flew his own plane to tournaments for over 50 years.

Jack Nicklaus designed more than 300 around the world.

Annika Sörenstam became the first woman to play in a PGA TOUR event in 58 years when she competed in the 2003 Bank of America Colonial.

Gary Player has claimed to have traveled more miles for sport than any athlete in history, an estimated 15 million miles.

Ben Hogan miraculously survived a head-on collision with a bus, an accident so severe that doctors said he might never walk again, let alone play golf; he went on to win six more majors.

Sam Snead won a tournament in six different decades, the only player ever to achieve such longevity.

Seve Ballesteros won The Open Championship in 1979 at Royal Lytham & St Annes with a parking lot shot, one of the most famous shots in golf history.

Lee Trevino was struck by lightning at the 1975 Western Open, survived, and went on to win many more tournaments.

Nancy Lopez won five consecutive tournaments during her first full season on the LPGA Tour in 1978, a feat unmatched in women's golf.

Phil Mickelson is known for hitting a moving ball on the green during the 2018 U.S. Open, a controversial act that shocked the golf world.

Walter Hagen was famous for arriving at tournaments in a chauffeur-driven limousine and changing his shoes in the parking lot, exuding style and confidence.

Byron Nelson once made 113 consecutive cuts over a span of several years, a record that stood until Tiger Woods broke it in 2003.

Tom Watson nearly won The Open Championship at the age of 59, which would have made him the oldest major champion by over a decade.

Mickey Wright possessed, according to Ben Hogan and Byron Nelson, the best golf swing they ever saw.

Gene Sarazen invented the modern sand wedge and debuted it at the British Open, which he won.

Babe Didrikson Zaharias was the first American to win the British Women's Amateur and qualified for the men's PGA TOUR, competing in three events.

Julius Boros remains the oldest winner of a major championship, capturing the 1968 PGA Championship at 48 years old.

Betsy Rawls overcame a serious automobile accident early in her career to become one of the winningest players in LPGA history.

Nick Faldo spent a staggering 98 weeks as the World No. 1 golfer from 1990 to 1994.

Sandy Lyle was the first golfer to win The Open Championship with a birdie on the final hole in over 60 years when he did so in 1985.

Pat Bradley is one of the few golfers to have won all four majors recognized by the LPGA at the time of her playing career.

Raymond Floyd won his first PGA TOUR event and his last, 22 years apart, on the same golf course (Doral Country Club in Miami).

Lorena Ochoa retired at the age of 28 while she was the top-ranked female golfer in the world.

Johnny Miller is known for his final round of 63 at the 1973 U.S. Open, the lowest score to win a major championship until it was tied by Henrik Stenson at the 2016 Open Championship.

Hale Irwin is the most successful player in Senior PGA Tour history, with 45 wins including 7 senior majors.

Greg Norman spent 331 weeks as the world's number one golfer in the 1980s and 1990s.

Chi Chi Rodriguez grew up in poverty and started as a caddie, eventually becoming famous for using his putter as a "sword" to celebrate his victories.

Karrie Webb is the youngest woman to complete the Career Grand Slam in golf.

Ian Poulter helped inspire one of the greatest comebacks in Ryder Cup history, known as the "Miracle at Medinah," in 2012.

Ernie Els founded a charitable foundation focused on supporting individuals with autism, inspired by his son who is affected by the condition.

Fred Couples earned the nickname "Boom Boom" for his ability to hit long drives off the tee.

Payne Stewart won the U.S. Open in 1999 and tragically died in a plane crash four months later; he is remembered for his distinctive knickerbockers.

Zach Johnson won the 2007 Masters with a strategic game plan that avoided taking on any of the par-5s in two, contrary to the usual aggressive approach.

Yani Tseng became the youngest golfer ever, male or female, to win five major championships at the age of 22.

Jordan Spieth won the 2015 Masters and U.S. Open before turning 22, joining Tiger Woods as the only players to win multiple majors before that age.

Rory McIlroy won the 2011 U.S. Open with a record-breaking 16-under-par score, the lowest in U.S. Open history.

Inbee Park won the 2013 Women's PGA Championship to become the youngest player to win three different majors.

Brooke Henderson is the youngest player to win a professional golf tour event, doing so at the age of 14 in a Canadian Women's Tour event.

Justin Rose secured golf's return to the Olympics by winning the gold medal at the 2016 Rio Games, the first since 1904.

Dustin Johnson dominated the 2020 Masters with a record 20-under-par, the lowest score in the history of the tournament.

Sergio Garcia finally won his first major at the Masters in 2017, after 73 previous attempts, in a dramatic playoff.

Adam Scott ended Australia's long wait for a Masters champion with his victory in 2013, using a long putter.

Lydia Ko became the youngest ever winner of an LPGA Tour event at 15 years and 4 months old.

Bubba Watson won the 2012 Masters with a miraculous hook shot from the trees on the second playoff hole.

Collin Morikawa made history by winning the PGA Championship on his debut in 2020, showcasing an extraordinary level of composure and skill for a newcomer.

Henrik Stenson became the first Swedish male golfer to win a major, clinching the 2016 Open Championship at Royal Troon in a legendary duel with Phil Mickelson, finishing 20-under-par, the lowest score relative to par in Open history.

Tommy Fleetwood set the record for the lowest score in U.S. Open history at a single round with a 63 during the final round at Shinnecock Hills in 2018, showcasing his exceptional talent and precision under pressure.

Moe Norman, known for his eccentric personality and unparalleled accuracy, is often regarded as the best ball-striker in the history of golf. His mastery of the game and unique swing, dubbed "The Single Plane Swing," earned him the respect of his peers and golf enthusiasts alike.

Michelle Wie West became the youngest player to qualify for a USGA amateur championship at the age of 10 and later, at 14, became the youngest winner of the U.S. Women's Amateur Public Links and the youngest to qualify for an LPGA Tour event.

Chichi Rodríguez once fought off a mugger with a putter during a tournament, showcasing not only his golfing skills but also his courage.

Vijay Singh, from Fiji, worked as a bouncer before becoming one of the top golfers in the world, proving his diverse skill set both on and off the course.

Bryson DeChambeau is known for his scientific approach to golf, using single-length irons and focusing on physics to improve his game, earning him the nickname "The Scientist."

Lee Elder broke barriers as the first African American to play in the Masters Tournament in 1975, paving the way for future generations of golfers.

Young Tom Morris is the youngest player ever to win a major, securing the Open Championship at the tender age of 17.

Francis Ouimet's victory in the 1913 U.S. Open as an amateur is considered one of the greatest upsets in sports history, significantly boosting golf's popularity in the United States.

JoAnne Carner earned the nickname "Big Mama" for her powerful drive and became one of the first women to compete in a PGA TOUR event.

John Daly won the 1991 PGA Championship as the ninth alternate, making one of the most surprising victories in golf history.

Ai Miyazato, from Japan, became the first Asian golfer to be ranked No. 1 in the Women's World Golf Rankings in 2010.

Norman Xiong has been touted as the next big thing in golf since his amateur days, drawing comparisons to Tiger Woods for his talent and early success.

Sharmila Nicollet from India is known not only for her achievements on the course but also for being a trailblazer in Indian women's golf.

Calvin Peete overcame a late start in golf and a physical disability to become the most accurate driver in the PGA TOUR during the 1980s.

Patty Berg was a founding member and leading figure of the LPGA, winning a record 15 major championships in her career.

Hideki Matsuyama made history as the first Japanese male to win a golf major, capturing the 2021 Masters Tournament.

Mickey Wright's powerful swing was so admired that Ben Hogan himself said it was the best he'd ever seen.

Laura Davies is known for her long drive and has won 85 professional tournaments worldwide, including four majors.

Charlie Sifford broke the color barrier in golf, becoming the first African American to play on the PGA TOUR.

Nancy Lopez won the LPGA Rookie of the Year, Player of the Year, and the Vare Trophy for lowest scoring average in her first full season (1978).

Althea Gibson was the first African American woman to compete on the women's professional golf tour in 1964.

Jason Day rose to World No. 1 in the Official World Golf Ranking, having overcome a difficult childhood and early financial hardships.

Retief Goosen survived a lightning strike while playing golf as an amateur, which nearly ended his career before it began.

Betsy King is known for her philanthropy as much as her golf, building houses in Africa through her charity work.

Tommy Armour nicknamed "The Silver Scot," won three majors and later became a renowned instructor, authoring a classic book on golf instruction.

Kathy Whitworth holds the record for the most wins in LPGA history, with 88 career victories.

Fuzzy Zoeller is one of the few golfers to win the Masters on his first attempt, achieving the feat in 1979.

J.H. Taylor is one of the pioneers of the modern game of golf, winning The Open Championship five times in the early 20th century.

Isao Aoki became the first Japanese player to win a PGA TOUR event, doing so in 1983.

Jan Stephenson was a leading figure in women's golf in the 1970s and 1980s, known for her winning skills and charismatic personality.

Lanny Wadkins won the 1977 PGA Championship and was known for his competitive spirit, playing on eight Ryder Cup teams.

Meg Mallon won four major championships and was known for her exceptional putting skills.

Ken Venturi overcame severe dehydration to win the 1964 U.S. Open in dramatic fashion.

K.J. Choi is the first Korean to win on the PGA TOUR, opening the door for many Asian golfers.

Juli Inkster has had a long and successful career, including winning seven majors and playing in nine Solheim Cups.

Curtis Strange became the first player since Ben Hogan to win back-to-back U.S. Open titles in 1988 and 1989.

Suzann Pettersen won the Solheim Cup for Europe with a clutch putt in 2019, shortly before announcing her retirement from professional golf.

Rory Sabbatini changed his citizenship to Slovakian to help grow the game in his wife's home country and to compete in the Olympics.

Christina Kim is known for her vibrant personality and expressive style on the course, making her a fan favorite.

Paula Creamer won the 2010 U.S. Women's Open with a 12-foot birdie putt on the final hole, securing her victory by four strokes.

Babe Zaharias was not only a golf champion but also an Olympic track and field athlete, showcasing her versatile athletic talent.

Sergio Garcia finally won his first major at the Masters in 2017, after 73 previous attempts, in a dramatic playoff against Justin Rose.

Lorena Ochoa decided to retire at the top of her game, leaving as the world's number one female golfer in 2010.

Justin Thomas won the PGA Championship in 2017, and his grandfather and father were both PGA professionals, making golf a family tradition.

Annika Sörenstam made a comeback to LPGA Tour competition in 2021 after retiring in 2008, showing her enduring passion for the game.

Billy Casper was known for his exceptional putting skills and won 51 PGA TOUR events, including three majors.

Judy Rankin overcame scoliosis to become one of the leading figures in women's golf and a respected golf broadcaster.

Greg Norman's aggressive play and entrepreneurial spirit have made him one of the most recognizable figures in golf.

Harold Varner III became one of the few African American golfers to earn a PGA TOUR card, advocating for diversity in golf with his inspiring journey from a modest background.

Tony Finau scored a hole-in-one during the Par 3 Contest at the 2018 Masters Tournament and famously dislocated his ankle while celebrating, only to pop it back into place and continue playing.

Charley Hoffman donated his entire paycheck from the 2017 Shriners Hospitals for Children Open to the victims of the Las Vegas shooting, showcasing his generous spirit beyond the golf course.

Nelly Korda won the Olympic Gold in golf for the USA at the Tokyo 2020 Olympics, following in the athletic footsteps of her tennis-playing parents and professional golfer sister.

Jean van de Velde's disastrous triple-bogey on the 18th hole at Carnoustie in the 1999 Open Championship is one of the most dramatic collapses in golf history, famously removing his shoes and socks to consider playing a shot from the Barry Burn.

John Daly's quote after winning the 1991 PGA Championship, "I believe in fate. I believe that everything happens for a reason, but I think it's important to seek out that reason; that's how you learn," captures his philosophical approach to life and golf.

Angela Stanford won her first major at the 2018 Evian Championship after over 18 years on the LPGA Tour, proving that persistence and hard work eventually pay off.

Padraig Harrington decided to rebuild his swing after winning back-to-back British Opens in 2007 and 2008, a rare move for a golfer at the peak of his career.

Tom Kite endured heartbreak at the U.S. Open several times before finally winning in 1992 at Pebble Beach, known for its challenging conditions, including a gusty final round.

Rory McIlroy's victory at the 2014 PGA Championship at Valhalla was clinched in near darkness, a testament to his determination to finish the round despite fading light.

Jordan Spieth's remarkable recovery shot from the practice range during the final round of the 2017 Open Championship at Royal Birkdale is one of the most memorable moments in recent golf history.

Moe Norman was quoted saying, "I don't know where the self is, but I know where the ball is," highlighting his unique perspective on golf and life.

Xander Schauffele won the gold medal in golf at the Tokyo 2020 Olympics, overcoming the challenges of the pandemic-affected season.

Beth Daniel's emotional victory at the 1990 Mazda LPGA Championship came after several years of struggles and adjustments to her game, showcasing her resilience.

Davis Love III captained the winning 2016 Ryder Cup team, a redemption after the heartbreaking loss in 2012 at Medinah.

Stewart Cink won the 2009 Open Championship at Turnberry, but the event is perhaps best remembered for Tom Watson's near-victory at the age of 59.

Suzy Whaley qualified for the 2003 Greater Hartford Open, becoming the first woman in 58 years to qualify for a PGA TOUR event, challenging gender norms in the sport.

Doug Sanders missed a 3-foot putt on the 72nd hole of the 1970 Open Championship at St. Andrews, leading to a playoff loss to Jack Nicklaus, a moment that defined his career.

Lexi Thompson faced a controversial four-stroke penalty at the 2017 ANA Inspiration, which was pointed out by a television viewer, sparking debate about viewer call-ins.

Ian Woosnam discovered he had one too many clubs in his bag during the final round of the 2001 Open Championship, incurring a penalty that dashed his chances of contention.

Brandel Chamblee transitioned from PGA TOUR player to one of the most outspoken and analytical golf commentators on television, often sparking debate with his views.

Ben Crenshaw's emotional victory at the 1995 Masters came just days after the death of his mentor, Harvey Penick, making it one of the most heartfelt moments in golf.

Michelle Wie's powerful driving and early promise led her to turn professional just before her 16th birthday, amidst immense media attention and high expectations.

Hale Irwin's victory at the 1990 U.S. Open at Medinah came at the age of 45, making him one of the oldest winners of the championship.

Gary Woodland won the 2019 U.S. Open at Pebble Beach and celebrated with Amy Bockerstette, a young golfer with Down syndrome he had formed a heartwarming bond with during a practice round at the Phoenix Open.

Lucas Glover's wife, Krista, was arrested for domestic violence in 2018, an off-the-course incident that brought unexpected attention to the usually private golfer.

Bev Norwood, a renowned golf journalist and publicist, was instrumental in shaping the public images of many golf legends, working behind the scenes to promote the sport.

Darren Clarke's emotional victory at the 2011 Open Championship was a tribute to his late wife, Heather, who had died of cancer five years prior, showcasing the personal struggles golfers often face.

Camilo Villegas performed his signature "Spider-Man" pose to read greens, a unique method that endeared him to fans for its originality and athleticism.

Bubba Watson adopted a pink driver in support of cancer research, demonstrating his commitment to causes off the golf course.

Tiger Woods' "Better than most" putt on the 17th hole at TPC Sawgrass during the 2001 Players Championship is one of the most iconic shots in golf, accompanied by the memorable call from announcer Gary Koch.

Annika Sörenstam's pioneering decision to compete in the 2003 Bank of America Colonial on the PGA TOUR challenged the norms of professional golf and inspired future generations of female golfers.

Se Ri Pak's victory at the 1998 U.S. Women's Open at Blackwolf Run is credited with inspiring a whole generation of Korean female golfers, leading to a surge in the sport's popularity in South Korea.

Keegan Bradley faced significant scrutiny and pressure after winning the 2011 PGA Championship due to his use of a long putter, which later became a center of controversy in the golfing world.

Graeme McDowell ended a 40-year drought for European golfers at the U.S. Open with his win in 2010 at Pebble Beach, highlighting the shifting balance of power in international golf.

Harold Varner III made history as the first African American golfer to earn full playing privileges on the PGA Tour of Australasia.

Stacy Lewis donated her entire $195,000 winner's check from the 2017 Cambia Portland Classic to Hurricane Harvey relief efforts, directly supporting the recovery in her hometown of Houston, Texas.

Bernhard Langer famously missed a six-foot putt on the 18th hole of the 1991 Ryder Cup, a miss that resulted in the United States retaining the cup, in what became known as "The War by the Shore."

Michelle Wie West, at the age of 13, became the youngest player to make an LPGA cut at the 2003 Kraft Nabisco Championship, showcasing early on her exceptional talent.

Rory McIlroy won the 2011 U.S. Open with a record-breaking total score of 268, beating the previous record by four strokes, just months after a final-round collapse at the Masters.

Moe Norman, revered for his ball-striking, claimed, "I've never lost a golf ball in my life," highlighting his unparalleled accuracy and control.

Annika Sörenstam received a personal invitation from Arnold Palmer to play in the PGA Tour's Bay Hill Invitational in 2004, a rare honor for a female golfer.

Billy Casper chose to lay up on the par-3 16th hole all four rounds of the 1959 U.S. Open, a strategic decision that contributed significantly to his victory.

Bubba Watson broke down in tears during his victory speech after winning his first Masters in 2012, dedicating the win to his family and recently adopted son.

Lexi Thompson faced a controversial four-stroke penalty during the final round of the 2017 ANA Inspiration, a major moment that sparked widespread debate about viewer call-ins.

Brooks Koepka became the first golfer in the modern era to win two U.S. Opens and two PGA Championships in consecutive years (2017-2018 U.S. Open, 2018-2019 PGA Championship).

Ben Hogan's quote after his 1950 U.S. Open win at Merion, following a near-fatal car accident, resonates widely: "I'm glad I brought this course, this monster, to its knees."

Gene Sarazen hit "the shot heard 'round the world" at the 1935 Masters, a double eagle from the fairway on the 15th hole, catapulting him to a playoff victory.

Nancy Lopez won nine tournaments in her sophomore season of 1978, including five consecutive wins, setting a standard for dominance on the LPGA Tour.

Se Ri Pak's win at the 1998 U.S. Women's Open inspired an entire generation of South Korean women to pursue professional golf, fundamentally changing the landscape of the sport.

Gary Player famously said, "The harder I practice, the luckier I get," emphasizing the importance of hard work in golf success.

Tom Watson and Jack Nicklaus had a historic "Duel in the Sun" at the 1977 Open Championship, with Watson edging out Nicklaus by one stroke in one of golf's greatest battles.

Ian Poulter rallied the European team at the 2012 Ryder Cup with a series of clutch putts, helping stage a remarkable comeback known as the "Miracle at Medinah."

Jordan Spieth's 2015 Masters win included a record-tying 18-under par performance, announcing his arrival as a major force in golf.

Sandy Lyle hit a 7-iron shot from a fairway bunker on the 18th hole to clinch the 1988 Masters, one of the most memorable shots in tournament history.

Tiger Woods' "Better than most!" putt on the 17th green at the 2001 Players Championship remains one of the most iconic calls and moments in golf broadcasting.

Zach Johnson used what he described as "his grit" to win the 2015 Open Championship at St. Andrews, prevailing in a playoff against Louis Oosthuizen and Marc Leishman.

Padraig Harrington won back-to-back British Opens in 2007 and 2008, then added the PGA Championship in 2008, becoming the first European to win three majors in two years since 1908.

Phil Mickelson jumped in the air after making an 18-foot birdie putt on the 18th hole to win the 2004 Masters, his first major victory, in what became an iconic image.

Henrik Stenson and Phil Mickelson's final round battle at the 2016 Open Championship is often compared to the "Duel in the Sun," with Stenson coming out on top.

Justin Thomas recorded the 9th sub-60 round in PGA Tour history at the 2017 Sony Open in Hawaii, shooting a 59.

Jason Day's emotional victory in the 2015 PGA Championship was punctuated by tears, as he broke through for his first major win with a record-setting 20-under-par total.

Keegan Bradley surprised the golf world by winning the 2011 PGA Championship, becoming only the third player in history to win a major on his first attempt.

Angel Cabrera won the 2007 U.S. Open and 2009 Masters, becoming the first South American to win both tournaments.

Tommy Armour III once remarked, "Golf is an awkward set of bodily contortions designed to produce a graceful result," highlighting the unique challenges of the sport.

Tony Finau overcame a dislocated ankle during the Par-3 Contest to finish in the top 10 of the 2018 Masters, showcasing remarkable resilience and determination.

Cristie Kerr became an advocate for breast cancer awareness and fundraising efforts after her mother was diagnosed with the disease, blending her personal and professional life in meaningful ways.

Ernie Els won the 2012 British Open and then donated a significant portion of his winnings to his foundation supporting autism, inspired by his son's condition.

Laura Davies was knighted by Queen Elizabeth II, recognizing her contributions to golf and becoming one of the few golfers to receive such an honor.

Chi Chi Rodriguez's quote, "When a man retires, his wife gets twice the husband but only half the income," humorously reflects on retirement from professional golf.

Dustin Johnson dominated the 2020 Masters, winning by five strokes and setting the tournament scoring record with a total of 268, 20-under-par.

Rickie Fowler celebrated his first PGA Tour win at the 2012 Wells Fargo Championship by beating Rory McIlroy and D.A. Points in a playoff, establishing himself as one of golf's most promising talents.

Lydia Ko became the youngest ever World No. 1 in professional golf at age 17, shattering previous records and setting a new benchmark for early success in the sport.

Nick Price was known for his rapid play and precision, with a victory at the 1994 PGA Championship where he set a then-record margin of victory with a six-stroke win over Corey Pavin.

Inbee Park completed the Career Grand Slam with her win at the 2015 Ricoh Women's British Open, joining an elite group of female golfers to achieve this feat.

Charley Hoffman's generosity was on full display when he donated his entire paycheck from the 2017 Shriners Hospitals for Children Open to the victims of the Las Vegas shooting.

Paula Creamer's dramatic 75-foot eagle putt to win the 2014 HSBC Women's Champions in a playoff is one of the most memorable shots in LPGA history.

Darren Clarke's emotional victory at the 2011 Open Championship was a heartfelt moment, as he dedicated his win to his late wife, who had died of cancer.

Sergio Garcia finally won his first major at the 2017 Masters after years of near-misses, in what was a popular victory for one of golf's most enduring talents.

Francesco Molinari became the first Italian to win a major, clinching the 2018 Open Championship with a spectacular display of golf, especially in the final rounds.

Cameron Champ is known not only for his extraordinary driving distance but also for his activism and efforts to promote diversity in golf.

Jim Furyk shot a PGA Tour record 58 during the final round of the 2016 Travelers Championship, marking the lowest round ever recorded in a PGA Tour event.

Martin Kaymer's dominant performance to win the 2014 U.S. Open at Pinehurst by eight strokes showcased his precision and control under pressure.

Tommy Bolt was famous for his fiery temper and once threw his entire bag into a lake, earning him the nickname "Thunder" and illustrating the emotional challenges of the game.

Jean Van de Velde's tragic collapse on the 18th hole of the 1999 Open Championship remains one of the most unforgettable moments in golf, a cautionary tale of victory slipping away.

Yani Tseng's remarkable achievement of winning five major championships before the age of 23 set her apart as one of the most talented female golfers in history.

John Daly's win at the 1991 PGA Championship as a ninth alternate is one of the sport's greatest Cinderella stories, showcasing the unpredictable nature of golf.

Lorena Ochoa retired at the peak of her career, a rare decision that left fans wondering what more she could have achieved had she continued playing.

Zach Johnson's strategic play to win the 2007 Masters, especially his decision to lay up on all the par-5s, is a masterclass in playing to one's strengths.

Hale Irwin's 45-foot birdie putt on the 72nd hole of the 1990 U.S. Open to force a playoff, which he won, is one of the most clutch moments in major championship history.

Jason Day's emotional victory in the 2015 PGA Championship was made even more poignant as he battled vertigo symptoms throughout the season.

Rory McIlroy's record-breaking win at the 2011 U.S. Open by eight strokes, just weeks after a Masters meltdown, was a stunning display of resilience and talent.

Annika Sörenstam's 59 in the second round of the 2001 Standard Register PING remains the only sub-60 round in LPGA Tour history.

Justin Rose's gold medal win in golf's return to the Olympics in 2016, over a century since it was last included, highlighted the sport's global appeal and competition.

Lee Trevino survived being struck by lightning during the 1975 Western Open, a dramatic reminder of the dangers professional golfers sometimes face.

Kathy Whitworth's 88 career wins on the LPGA Tour set a standard for excellence and longevity that has yet to be surpassed.

Michelle Wie's powerful drive and precocious talent made her one of the most hyped and watched players from a very young age.

Billy Horschel showed remarkable sportsmanship by conceding a lengthy putt to Rory McIlroy during the singles matches of the 2014 Ryder Cup, embodying the spirit of the game.

Seve Ballesteros' imaginative play and charismatic presence made him a fan favorite and a symbol of European golf's rise in the late 20th century.

Brooke Henderson broke the Canadian record for most wins on the LPGA or PGA Tours, showcasing her country's growing influence in the sport.

Ian Woosnam discovered he had 15 clubs in his bag during the final round of the 2001 Open Championship, a mistake that cost him a two-stroke penalty and likely the championship.

Mo Martin's eagle on the 72nd hole of the 2014 Women's British Open, using a fairway wood from the fairway, secured her only major victory in dramatic fashion.

Jordan Spieth's near wire-to-wire victory at the 2015 Masters set several records and announced his arrival as a major force in golf.

Augusta National Golf Club (USA) – Home of The Masters, Augusta is known for its azaleas and Amen Corner, the crucial trio of holes from 11 to 13 that often decide the tournament.

St Andrews Old Course (Scotland) – Considered the "Home of Golf," it's famous for the Swilcan Bridge on the 18th hole, a historic crossing for many legends of the game.

Pebble Beach Golf Links (USA) – Offers some of the most stunning seaside views in golf, particularly at the 7th hole, one of the most photographed in the world.

Royal County Down Golf Club (Northern Ireland) – Known for its rugged beauty and the Mourne Mountains backdrop, it's a natural links course favored for its challenging layout.

Pine Valley Golf Club (USA) – Frequently topping lists of the world's best courses, Pine Valley is celebrated for its architectural purity and isolated fairways.

Golf Courses

Royal Melbourne Golf Club (Australia) – The West Course showcases Alister MacKenzie's brilliant bunkering, blending naturally with the Australian Sandbelt.

Shinnecock Hills Golf Club (USA) – One of the oldest incorporated clubs, it's recognized for hosting the second-ever U.S. Open and its traditional links-style layout.

Cypress Point Club (USA) – Offers the dramatic 16th hole, a long par-3 over the Pacific Ocean, one of the most iconic holes in golf.

Royal Dornoch Golf Club (Scotland) – Revered for its raised putting greens and wild gorse, it's a classic Scottish links without a single tree on the course.

Oakmont Country Club (USA) – Known for its "Church Pews" bunker between the 3rd and 4th holes, Oakmont is one of the toughest tests in golf.

Muirfield (Scotland) – A historic venue that has hosted The Open Championship numerous times, it's known for its unique circular layout ensuring the wind direction changes on every hole.

The Old Head Golf Links (Ireland) – Perched on a dramatic clifftop, it offers some of the most breathtaking views in golf, with nearly every hole overlooking the Atlantic Ocean.

Merion Golf Club (USA) – Site of Ben Hogan's famous 1-iron shot during the 1950 U.S. Open, Merion is celebrated for its strategic layout and wicker basket pin markers.

Royal Portrush Golf Club (Northern Ireland) – Host of the 2019 Open Championship, it's known for the Dunluce Links and its stunning coastal views.

Carnoustie Golf Links (Scotland) – Often referred to as "Carnasty" due to its difficulty, it's famed for its challenging finishing holes, particularly the 18th.

Winged Foot Golf Club (USA) - Known for its narrow fairways, thick rough, and slick greens, it's a perennial host for the U.S. Open, including the 2006 meltdown by Phil Mickelson on the 72nd hole.

Whistling Straits (USA) - With holes along two miles of Lake Michigan shoreline, it's known for its dramatic Pete Dye design and numerous bunkers.

Royal St. George's Golf Club (England) - The first course outside Scotland to host The Open, it's known for its undulating fairways and the deep bunker on the 4th hole.

Turnberry (Ailsa Course) (Scotland) - Famous for the "Duel in the Sun" between Tom Watson and Jack Nicklaus in the 1977 Open, it offers stunning views of Ailsa Craig.

Bethpage Black Course (USA) - A public course known for its warning sign on the first tee, emphasizing its difficulty and the physical demands it places on golfers.

Bandon Dunes Golf Resort (USA) – Offers multiple courses with true links-style play in the United States, with Bandon Dunes and Pacific Dunes often highlighted for their seaside beauty.

Kingsbarns Golf Links (Scotland) – Though relatively new, opened in 2000, it quickly became a must-play course, known for its beautiful vistas over the North Sea.

Le Golf National (Albatros Course) (France) – Host of the 2018 Ryder Cup, known for its stadium-like design and water hazards, particularly on the closing holes.

Kiawah Island (Ocean Course) (USA) – Host of the 1991 Ryder Cup ("The War by the Shore"), it's recognized for being one of the most challenging courses, with winds coming off the Atlantic.

Royal Birkdale Golf Club (England) – Known for its towering sand dunes and hosting numerous major championships, including The Open.

Quivira Golf Club (Mexico) – Offers dramatic oceanfront holes and cliffside views, particularly the 5th and 6th holes, which are played atop sheer cliffs above the Pacific.

Royal Liverpool Golf Club (Hoylake) (England) – Historic links known for its strategic play; Tiger Woods famously used his driver only once en route to winning the 2006 Open Championship here.

Golf National Albatros Course (France) – Famous for its role in the 2018 Ryder Cup, particularly the closing holes which created a natural amphitheater for spectators.

National Golf Links of America (USA) – Charles Blair Macdonald's masterpiece, known for holes inspired by famous British and Scottish designs, creating a "museum" of classic golf architecture.

Royal Lytham & St Annes Golf Club (England) – Known for its 206 bunkers, making strategic play essential, and its history of hosting major championships, including the Open.

Cruden Bay Golf Club (Scotland) – Offers stunning views and unique holes, like the blind par-3 4th hole, amidst the dunes on Scotland's northeast coast.

Streamsong Resort (Red Course) (USA) – Set on a former phosphate mine, this course features dramatic elevation changes and a unique inland links feel in central Florida.

Cabot Cliffs (Canada) – Located in Nova Scotia, it's celebrated for its cliff-top holes, especially the par-3 16th, which plays over a canyon to a green perched on a cliff edge.

Cape Wickham Links (Australia) – Known for having more ocean view holes than any other course in the Southern Hemisphere, offering a true links experience on King Island.

Ganton Golf Club (England) – Situated inland, Ganton offers a links-like challenge with its fast-running fairways and deep pot bunkers, a rarity away from the coast.

Royal Troon Golf Club (Old Course) (Scotland) - Host of the "Postage Stamp" 8th hole, one of the shortest but most challenging par-3s in major championship golf.

Lahinch Golf Club (Ireland) - Known for its "Klondyke" (5th) and "Dell" (4th) holes, unique due to blind shots and natural dune landscapes, making it a classic links test.

Royal Adelaide Golf Club (Australia) - Features the unique use of the local railway line as an integral part of its design, affecting several holes along the course.

Kauri Cliffs (New Zealand) - Offers panoramic ocean views from 15 of its 18 holes, set atop cliffs above the Bay of Islands, making it one of the most picturesque courses in the world.

The Ocean Course at Kiawah Island (USA) - Renowned for hosting the "War by the Shore" 1991 Ryder Cup, it's known for being one of the most difficult courses due to its exposure to Atlantic winds.

Fancourt (The Links) (South Africa) – Designed by Gary Player, The Links is considered one of the finest golf courses in the world, replicating a Scottish Links course in South Africa.

Dismal River (White Course) (USA) – A Jack Nicklaus signature design set in the Nebraska sandhills, offering a challenging yet visually stunning golf experience.

Ballybunion Golf Club (Old Course) (Ireland) – Celebrated for its towering dunes and historic setting, Tom Watson praised it highly, enhancing its global reputation.

Sentosa Golf Club (Serapong Course) (Singapore) – Known for hosting the Singapore Open, the Serapong course offers stunning city skyline views and a challenging championship layout.

Ellerston Golf Course (Australia) – An exclusive, private course designed by Greg Norman, known for its privacy and challenging design, rarely seen by the public.

Wentworth Club (West Course) (England) - Host of the annual BMW PGA Championship, it's famous for its Burma Road nickname and challenging closing holes.

Casa de Campo (Teeth of the Dog) (Dominican Republic) - Pete Dye's oceanfront masterpiece, known for its signature holes that run along the Caribbean Sea.

Pasatiempo Golf Club (USA) - A Dr. Alister MacKenzie design, it's a public course offering a private club experience with its challenging holes and historical significance.

The European Club (Ireland) - Known for its rugged beauty and challenging links layout, it features 20 holes for a unique golfing experience.

Durban Country Club (South Africa) - Offers a mix of links and parkland holes, known for its history of hosting the South African Open and its undulating fairways.

Interlachen Country Club (USA) – Famous for Bobby Jones' "lily pad" shot during the 1930 U.S. Open, a pivotal moment on his way to the Grand Slam.

Royal Montreal Golf Club (Blue Course) (Canada) – The oldest golf club in North America, known for its challenging blue course that hosted the 2007 Presidents Cup.

Prestwick Golf Club (Scotland) – The birthplace of the Open Championship, known for its "Alps" hole and deep bunkers, filled with history and tradition.

The Grove (England) – Known for hosting the WGC-American Express Championship in 2006, it's one of the UK's finest luxury golf resorts, blending modern amenities with challenging golf.

Gleneagles (PGA Centenary Course) (Scotland) – Host of the 2014 Ryder Cup, known for its scenic beauty and Jack Nicklaus design, offering a modern test in a historic setting.

Sunningdale Golf Club (Old Course) (England) – A quintessential English heathland course, known for its natural beauty and strategic design, offering a pure golf experience.

Punta Espada Golf Club (Dominican Republic) – A Jack Nicklaus signature design, it's celebrated for its Caribbean vistas and has been voted the best golf course in the Caribbean and Mexico.

The Jockey Club (Red Course) (Argentina) – Designed by Alister MacKenzie, it's one of South America's premier golf venues, known for its challenging layout and prestigious history.

Pinehurst No. 2 (USA) – Host of several U.S. Opens, it's known for its crowned, undulating greens designed by Donald Ross, presenting a supreme test of precision and patience.

Tara Iti Golf Club (New Zealand) – An exclusive links course set among the dunes overlooking the Pacific Ocean, known for its minimalist design and stunning natural setting.

The Madison Club (USA) – Offers luxury golf in the California desert with a layout that includes water features and impeccable fairways, attracting celebrities and professional athletes.

Morfontaine Golf Club (France) – Esteemed for its exclusivity and the Vallière course, it's a masterpiece by Tom Simpson nestled in a serene forest setting, providing a sublime golf experience.

Sahalee Country Club (USA) – Known for its tight fairways flanked by towering cedar and fir trees, Sahalee's layout tested the world's best during the 1998 PGA Championship.

Royal Portrush Golf Club (Dunluce Course) (Northern Ireland) – The Dunluce Links, reimagined by Harry Colt, challenges golfers with its rugged coastal dunes and the infamous "Calamity Corner" 16th hole.

Victoria Golf Club (Australia) – Set on the Melbourne Sandbelt, it's celebrated for its strategic bunkering and fast, undulating greens, offering a classic test of golf.

Royal County Down Golf Club (Northern Ireland) - Offers the "Blind Man's Bluff" par-3 4th hole, emblematic of traditional links golf where the wind and visual deception play key roles.

TPC Sawgrass (Stadium Course) (USA) - Home to the iconic 17th hole "Island Green," this Pete Dye design is a bucket-list course for amateurs and a challenging venue for professionals.

Kawana Hotel Golf Course (Fuji Course) (Japan) - A Charles H. Alison design with stunning views of Mount Fuji, offering a scenic and strategic challenge.

Fishers Island Club (USA) - Accessible mainly by boat, this Seth Raynor design features breathtaking seaside holes and classic template holes adapted to its unique island setting.

Los Angeles Country Club (North Course) (USA) - Will host the U.S. Open in 2023, known for its Beverly Hills location and challenging layout that blends city views with traditional golf design.

Enniscrone Golf Club (Ireland) – Offers dramatic dune landscapes and a true links experience, highlighted by the challenging par-5 12th hole winding through the dunes.

Pinehurst No. 4 (USA) – Reimagined by Gil Hanse, it complements No. 2 with its own unique challenges, including restored sandy areas and natural topography.

Naruo Golf Club (Japan) – Esteemed for its history and challenging Kikuyu grass fairways, Naruo reflects classic Japanese golf design with strategic bunkering and fast greens.

The Country Club (Clyde/Squirrel Course) (USA) – Host of numerous significant tournaments, including the 1913 U.S. Open, it's known for its deep history and challenging layout in Brookline, Massachusetts.

LACC (Los Angeles Country Club) (USA) – The North Course is set to host the 2023 U.S. Open, noted for its recent Gil Hanse restoration that emphasized its golden-age design elements.

Golf Club Milano (Italy) – Nestled within Monza's Royal Park, it's known for its tight, tree-lined fairways and as a frequent Italian Open host, challenging Europe's best players.

Royal Cinque Ports Golf Club (England) – Known for its challenging links layout affected by the tidal changes, it's a historic Open Championship venue offering a stern test of golf.

Woking Golf Club (England) – A pioneer in strategic design, its influence on architecture, particularly the 4th hole's green complex, has been significant in golf history.

Prestwick Golf Club (Scotland) – Birthplace of The Open Championship, its "Cardinal Bunker" is among golf's most famous hazards, embodying the essence of links golf.

Machrihanish Golf Club (Scotland) – The opening hole requires a daring tee shot over the Atlantic Ocean, setting the tone for a classic Scottish links experience.

Portmarnock Golf Club (Ireland) – Known for its consistent quality across all 18 holes, it's a stern test when the wind whips across the narrow peninsula.

Royal Melbourne Golf Club (Composite Course) (Australia) – Combining the best holes from the East and West Courses, it's a regular host for the Presidents Cup, showcasing the finest of Australian sandbelt golf.

Hacienda Golf Club (USA) – Nestled in the rolling hills of La Habra Heights, California, it's known for its challenging elevation changes and classic design features.

Olympic Club (Lake Course) (USA) – Host of multiple U.S. Opens, it's notorious for its tight, tree-lined fairways and difficult, sloping greens, particularly the 18th.

Chambers Bay (USA) – Site of the 2015 U.S. Open, its fescue fairways and massive, undulating greens offered a unique test, drawing comparisons to British links courses.

Royal Liverpool Golf Club (England) - "Hoylake," as it's affectionately known, blends flat and dune-lined holes, requiring strategic play, highlighted by its demanding finish.

Walton Heath Golf Club (England) - Known for its heathland setting and as a Ryder Cup venue, its fast, firm fairways and heather-lined rough challenge the best.

St. George's Golf and Country Club (Canada) - A Stanley Thompson design known for its rolling terrain and strategic bunkering, it's a frequent Canadian Open host.

Sunningdale Golf Club (New Course) (England) - Complements its Old Course with a layout that's equally revered, known for its beautiful heathland setting and impeccable conditioning.

Valhalla Golf Club (USA) - Jack Nicklaus' design has hosted PGA Championships and a Ryder Cup, known for its risk-reward holes and dramatic finishing stretch.

Royal Porthcawl Golf Club (Wales) - Set against the Bristol Channel, it's Wales' premier course, offering a stern links challenge with spectacular sea views.

Western Gailes Golf Club (Scotland) - A classic links course that requires thoughtful navigation through dunes, pot bunkers, and the ever-present wind off the Firth of Clyde.

Barnbougle Dunes (Australia) - Set on Tasmania's rugged coastline, it's a modern classic, offering breathtaking ocean views and a true test of links golf.

Wentworth Club (East Course) (England) - Known for its heathland beauty and history as a Ryder Cup venue, the East Course offers a slightly more intimate golf experience compared to the West.

Pebble Beach Golf Links (USA) - The iconic coastal beauty and challenging play, especially during the U.S. Open, make it a bucket-list destination for golfers worldwide.

Tralee Golf Club (Ireland) – Designed by Arnold Palmer, Tralee is famed for its dramatic ocean views and the Palmer quote: "I may have designed the first nine, but surely God designed the back nine."

Carnegie Club at Skibo Castle (Scotland) – Offering exclusivity and luxury, this course is set in the Scottish Highlands and combines historical richness with a challenging layout.

The Honors Course (USA) – Located in Tennessee, it's known for its commitment to amateur golf and a challenging Pete Dye design that blends seamlessly with its natural surroundings.

Royal Zoute Golf Club (Belgium) – A links-style course located inland, Royal Zoute is known for its sandy soil, tight fairways, and strategic play, often described as Belgium's finest course.

Kapalua Resort (Plantation Course) (USA) – Host of the PGA Tour's Sentry Tournament of Champions, it's famous for its breathtaking ocean views and the dramatic, downhill 18th hole.

Rules & Gameplay

The First Known Rules: The first known rules of golf were drafted in 1744 for the Company of Gentlemen Golfers, now the Honourable Company of Edinburgh Golfers.

Maximum Club Rule: Golfers are limited to carrying a maximum of 14 clubs in their bag during a round, a rule established by the USGA and R&A in 1938.

Penalty Areas: Introduced in the 2019 rules update, "penalty areas" expanded the concept of water hazards to include areas like deserts and jungles, allowing golfers to ground their clubs.

The Anchoring Ban: In 2016, the USGA and R&A banned anchoring the club against the body while making a stroke, impacting players who used long putters.

Holing Out With a Flagstick: Since 2019, players can legally leave the flagstick in the hole while putting on the green, a change aimed at speeding up play.

Lost Ball Time: The search time for a lost ball was reduced from five minutes to three in 2019 to improve the pace of play.

Double Hit: Prior to 2019, if a golfer struck the ball twice in one swing, it resulted in a penalty. The rule change now counts it as a single stroke.

Accidental Movement on the Green: Rules now stipulate no penalty if a ball or ball-marker is accidentally moved on the putting green.

Dropping Procedure: The procedure for dropping a ball back in play now involves letting it go from knee height rather than shoulder height.

Embedded Ball Rule: The relief for an embedded ball is now more player-friendly, allowing for free relief in the general area, not just in the fairway.

Repairing Damage on the Green: Players can repair almost all damage on the green, including spike marks and animal damage, without penalty.

Out of Bounds Rule: Local rules may now allow for an alternative to stroke and distance for a ball that is lost or out of bounds, aimed at speeding up play.

Caddie Alignment: A new rule prevents caddies from standing behind a player to help with alignment during the setup.

The Spirit of the Game: Unlike many sports, golf heavily relies on player integrity, with rules expecting players to call penalties on themselves.

The "Stymie": Until 1952, if another ball blocked your putt on the green without being more than six inches away, you had to putt around or over it.

Animal Interference: A player may take relief without penalty if an animal (considered an "outside influence") moves their ball.

Ball Striking the Player: If your ball accidentally hits you after a stroke, there's no penalty, and the ball is played as it lies.

Wind-Moved Ball: If the wind moves your ball after addressing it, there used to be a penalty. Now, there's no penalty, and the ball is played from its new position.

Hitting Another Ball on the Green: If your ball hits another player's ball on the green, there's no penalty, but the struck ball must be replaced.

Snow and Natural Ice as Loose Impediments: Snow and natural ice, other than frost, are considered loose impediments and may be removed.

Artificial Devices: Using devices that gauge or measure slope or wind conditions is prohibited during play.

Provisional Ball for a Provisional Ball: It's possible to hit a provisional ball for your provisional ball if you believe the first one might be lost outside a penalty area or out of bounds.

Using Another Player's Club: You cannot use another player's club to make a stroke unless you're sharing clubs, which means staying within the 14-club limit together.

Wrong Scorecard Signature: If a golfer signs for a lower score than actually shot, they're disqualified. If they sign for a higher score, that score stands.

Disqualification for Late Arrival: Players can be disqualified for being late to their tee time, but rules have softened to allow a player to join the match within a certain time frame, usually five minutes, with penalties applied.

Advice: While seeking advice during a round is generally prohibited, players can ask for and give advice to their partner in team competitions.

Practice Between Holes: Practicing on or near the green of the last hole played is prohibited, but a rule change now allows for putting or chipping practice between holes if it doesn't delay play.

Moving Obstructions: Obstructions like rakes, bottles, etc., can be moved without penalty, but the ball must be replaced if it moves as a result.

Raking Bunkers: There's no specific rule on how to rake a bunker, but players are expected to leave the bunker in a better state than they found it for following golfers.

Ball Moves on the Green After Address: If the ball moves after the player has addressed it on the green, the player is no longer automatically deemed to have caused the ball to move.

Hitting the Wrong Ball: Playing the wrong ball results in a two-stroke penalty in stroke play or loss of hole in match play.

Dress Code: While not governed by the official rules of golf, many courses enforce a dress code, requiring collared shirts and banning denim or athletic shorts.

Altered Clubs: Using a club that has been purposely altered during a round is prohibited, except for adjustments made by natural forces.

Environmental Protection: Certain areas on the course may be designated as environmentally sensitive, and players are prohibited from entering or playing from these areas.

Ball at Rest Moved by Another Ball: If your ball at rest is moved by another ball in motion, you must replace your ball to its original position.

Ball Assisting or Interfering with Play: Players may request the lifting of a ball if it's believed to assist or interfere with another player's play.

Teeing Ground Boundaries: The player must tee the ball within the boundaries of the teeing ground, not in front of the tee markers, or they incur a penalty.

Dew and Frost: Dew and frost are not considered loose impediments or abnormal course conditions, meaning they cannot be removed or cleaned off a ball.

Leaf Rule: In autumn, local rules may allow a player to drop a ball without penalty if it's believed a leaf concealed it.

Sand Bottles on Carts: Players are encouraged to use sand bottles provided on carts to fill in divots, fostering course care and etiquette, although it's not an official rule of golf.

Committee's Discretion: Many rules allow for the Committee's discretion in enforcing penalties for breaches, ensuring fairness and consideration of unusual circumstances.

Embedded Ball in the Rough: The relief for an embedded ball was extended to the rough, not just the fairway, with the 2019 rules updates.

Club-Lengths: The standard for measuring relief areas is defined in terms of club-lengths, traditionally using the longest club in your bag, except the putter.

Tournament Committees: Can implement local rules for specific competitions, adjusting certain standard rules to accommodate unique course features or conditions.

Removing Dew or Frost on Your Line: Players are not allowed to manually remove dew or frost to clear a path on the putting green.

Accidentally Striking the Ball More than Once: Before 2019, accidentally hitting the ball more than once during a stroke incurred a penalty; now, it counts as only one stroke.

Sharing Clubs: Is allowed, provided the total number does not exceed 14 clubs, and it does not unduly delay play.

No Penalty for Moving Loose Impediments in a Bunker: Unlike previous rules, as of 2019, players can remove loose impediments in a bunker without penalty.

Unplayable Ball in a Bunker: Offers a player several relief options, including taking a drop outside the bunker with a two-stroke penalty.

Golf Balls with Different Playing Characteristics: A player may switch golf balls between the play of two holes unless the Committee has adopted the One Ball Rule for the competition.

The Original 13 Rules: Golf's earliest recorded rules from 1744 consisted of 13 basic principles, showcasing the game's simplicity and the importance of etiquette even in its infancy.

Golf Ball Evolution: Originally, golf balls were made of leather stuffed with feathers. The introduction of the gutta-percha ball in the mid-19th century revolutionized the game, offering better flight and durability.

The Mulligan: A "mulligan" allows a player to redo a bad shot and is not recognized in official rules but is a common courtesy in casual play. Its origins are debated, with various stories attributing its name to different individuals.

Hole Size Standardization: The standard golf hole size is 4.25 inches in diameter, a specification set in 1891 by the Royal & Ancient Golf Club of St Andrews to standardize play.

The 18-Hole Course: St Andrews is also credited with establishing the standard 18-hole course format in the mid-1700s, a model that golf courses worldwide follow today.

Tiger Tees: The term "Tiger Tees" refers to the back tees on a course, positioned to make the course more challenging, and are often used in professional tournaments.

Rub of the Green: This rule states that if a ball in motion is deflected or stopped by any outside agency (animal, opponent, etc.), the ball is played where it lies without penalty.

Golf in the Olympics: Golf was reintroduced in the 2016 Rio Olympics after a 112-year absence, highlighting the sport's global appeal and competition.

The Royal and Ancient Game: Often called "The Royal and Ancient Game," golf's rules are still governed by The Royal and Ancient Golf Club of St Andrews in Scotland, in partnership with the USGA.

First Professional Golfer: Allan Robertson is considered the first professional golfer, earning his living by making golf balls, playing matches, and teaching golf in the mid-19th century.

Biodegradable Golf Balls: To reduce environmental impact, especially in water hazards, biodegradable golf balls made from fish food or other materials have been developed.

The Color of Golf Balls: While white is traditional for visibility against green and blue backgrounds, golf balls come in various colors to enhance visibility in different playing conditions.

The Rarest Score: A "condor" is the rarest score, achieved by scoring four under par on a hole. This requires either a hole-in-one on a par-5 or a two on a par-6, both extremely rare occurrences.

Aces Wild: A "hole-in-one" is also called an "ace," a coveted achievement where the golfer gets the ball into the hole with one stroke from the tee.

The Term "Bogey": Originally, "bogey" was the term for the standard score for a hole, but it evolved to signify one over par, with "par" becoming the term for the expected score.

Night Golf: Some courses offer night golf, where the fairways, greens, and balls are illuminated, providing a unique golfing experience.

Golf on the Moon: Astronaut Alan Shepard famously hit two golf balls on the moon during the Apollo 14 mission in 1971, showcasing golf's universal appeal.

Handicap System: The handicap system, introduced in 1911, allows players of varying skill levels to compete on an equal footing by adjusting their score according to their ability.

The Green Jacket: Awarded to the winner of The Masters Tournament, the green jacket is one of golf's most famous traditions, symbolizing membership in the exclusive Augusta National Golf Club.

Drive for Show, Putt for Dough: This popular saying emphasizes the importance of putting. While long drives are impressive, games are often won on the green.

Oldest Golf Tournament: The Open Championship, first played in 1860 at Prestwick Golf Club in Scotland, is the oldest of golf's four major championships.

Caddie Origins: The term "caddie" comes from the French word "cadet," meaning a younger child or a student military officer, indicating someone who assists a golfer.

Golf During War: During WWII, British golf courses were often used for military purposes, including training and as defensive positions, with some even disguising bomb craters as sand traps.

Ladies' Golf Union: Founded in 1893, the Ladies' Golf Union was the first governing body in golf to specifically represent women players, promoting women's competitions and championships.

The "Silk Stocking Match": This historic match in 1926 featured amateur Bobby Jones and professional Walter Hagen, highlighting the growing popularity and competitiveness of professional golf.

First Golf Tee: The first patented tee was invented by Dr. George Grant in 1899, revolutionizing the game by elevating the ball for the initial shot, replacing the sand mounds previously used.

First Golf Tournament in the US: The first recorded golf tournament in the United States was held in 1895 under the auspices of the United States Golf Association (USGA).

Golf in Space: Golf is the only sport played on the moon, emphasizing its widespread appeal and the unique feats of astronauts.

The Solheim Cup: Similar to the Ryder Cup but for women, the Solheim Cup pits teams from Europe and the United States against each other, showcasing the best in women's golf.

Golf's Return to the Olympics: After a 112-year hiatus, golf made its Olympic comeback in 2016, underlining its global popularity and competitive spirit.

The Walker Cup: Named after George Herbert Walker, grandfather of U.S. President George H.W. Bush, this biennial event features amateur men from the US against those from Great Britain and Ireland.

The Claret Jug: Officially known as The Golf Champion Trophy, it is awarded to the winner of The Open Championship, one of golf's oldest and most prestigious tournaments.

Fore: Shouted as a warning when a ball is headed towards another person, its origins are debated but it's a crucial part of golf etiquette for safety.

Golf Simulator Popularity: With advancements in technology, golf simulators have become popular for training and entertainment, allowing play on virtual courses worldwide.

The Influence of Golf Architecture: The design of golf courses can significantly influence gameplay, with famous architects like Alister MacKenzie and Donald Ross shaping how golf is played.

First African-American PGA Member: In 1961, Charlie Sifford became the first African American to earn a PGA membership, breaking color barriers in professional golf.

The Ryder Cup: Begun in 1927, this biennial men's competition between teams from Europe and the United States is one of golf's most celebrated and intense team events.

Miniature Golf: Also known as "putt-putt," miniature golf is a fun variant with themed obstacles, making the game accessible and entertaining for all ages.

The FedEx Cup: Introduced in 2007, the FedEx Cup is a season-long points competition on the PGA Tour, culminating in a playoff system to determine the champion.

Presidential Golfers: Numerous U.S. Presidents have been avid golfers, with the game being a favored leisure activity among American leaders.

The Concept of Par: The term "par" represents the number of strokes a skilled golfer should take to complete a hole, considering both distance and obstacles.

Golf's Economic Impact: Beyond sport, golf is a significant economic driver, supporting jobs, tourism, and development worldwide.

Golfing Siblings: The Molinari brothers, Edoardo and Francesco, from Italy, are among the few siblings to have both played in the Ryder Cup, highlighting family talent in golf.

The Asian Tour: Established to promote professional golf in Asia, the Asian Tour has become a significant part of the global golf landscape, showcasing talent from the region.

Golf's Environmental Initiatives: Many golf courses implement sustainability practices, such as water conservation and habitat protection, to minimize their environmental footprint.

Famous Left-Handed Golfers: While most golfers play right-handed, left-handed players like Phil Mickelson have achieved significant success, challenging the norm.

Golf in Literature and Film: Golf has been featured in numerous books and movies, reflecting its cultural significance and the drama and humor inherent in the game.

Golf Swing Analytics: Modern technology allows for detailed analysis of golf swings, helping players improve through slow-motion videos and biomechanical data.

Unique Golf Tournaments: Some tournaments, like the Alfred Dunhill Links Championship, are played across multiple courses, adding a unique challenge and variety to the competition.

The Impact of Weather: Golf is uniquely affected by weather conditions, with wind, rain, and temperature influencing gameplay, strategy, and equipment choices.

Printed in Dunstable, United Kingdom